SCIENCE JOKES

GIFT BOOK

Illustrated

RALPH LANE

Ralph's gift books make great presents for birthdays, holidays, teacher appreciation, gift baskets, stocking stuffers, bathroom books, vacation books or just for the fun of it. Please consider leaving a review for this book on amazon.com or goodreads.com. You'll also want to read these other fine Ralph Lane books:

Dad Jokes Gift Book

Dad Jokes Halloween Gift Book

Dad Jokes Christmas Gift Book

Dad Jokes Valentine's Day Gift Book

Dad Jokes St. Patrick's Day Gift Book

Dad Jokes Easter Gift Book

Math Jokes Gift Book

Dad Jokes Birthday Gift Book

Sports Jokes Gift Book

Funny Jokes for Retired Folks

Get Well Chuckles Recovery Gift Book

Table of Contents

Atomic Bombs

What is a physicist's favorite food?

> fission chips

What do you call a circle of iron atoms at a carnival?

> a ferrous wheel

Two atoms are walking along. One of them says: "Oh no! I think I lost an electron!"

"Are you sure?"

"Yes, I'm positive."

Why can you never trust an atom?

They make up literally everything.

Why did the particle physicist go to the doctor?

Because he had an **atomic ache**!

What did the science student say when he heard the joke about two helium atoms?

He-He

A Dash of NaCl

Who is Iron Man's sidekick?

FEmale

I was reading a book on helium.

I couldn't put it down!

Why do chemists love nitrates so much?

They're cheaper than day rates.

What did the scientist say to the chemist whose lab smelled like rotten eggs?

"I'm sorry for your sulfuring."

Why was the molecule so calm?

It was in a stable relationship.

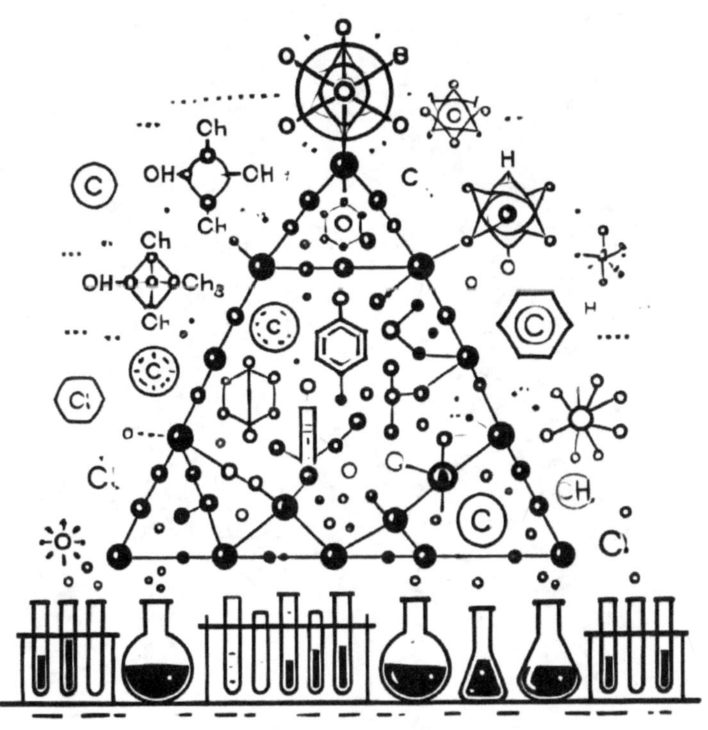

What do scientists put up in their living rooms at Christmas?

a chemis-tree

If a chemistry student knows absolutely nothing about Oxygen, does that make him an oxymoron?

Why are chemists good at solving problems?

They have all the solutions.

Why is combining a proton and an electron to make a neutron so popular?

It's free of charge.

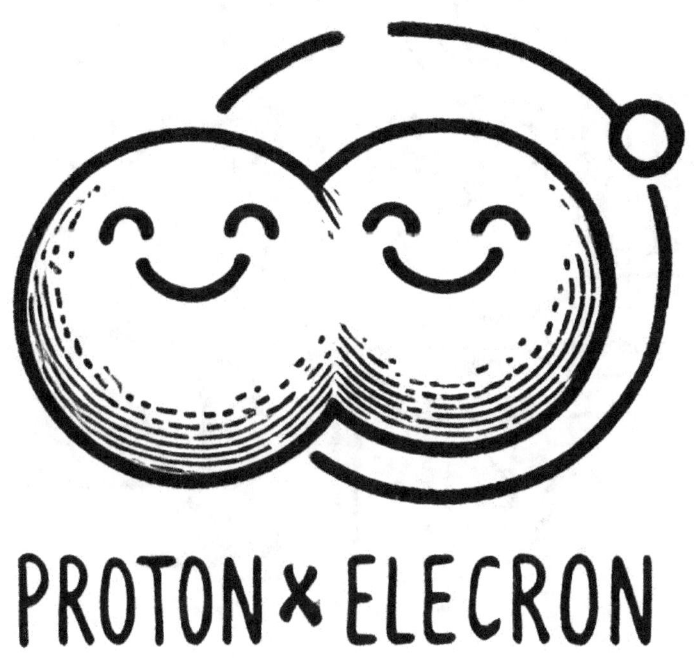

What type of fish is made out of 2 sodium atoms?

2 Na

Why do elements make terrible friends?

They're always reacting.

Two hydrogen atoms are walking down the street together when suddenly one shouts, "Darn it! I lost my electron!"

The other atom asks, "Are you sure?"

"Yes," it says. "I'm positive."

Beastly Funny

What type of do<u>gs</u> do chemists own?

laboratory retrievers

What do you call a dog who spends all his time in the laboratory scribbling pictures of his male buddies?

a lab-bro-doodle

Why did the amoeba fail its math test?

Because it multiplied by dividing.

Why did the white bear dissolve in water?

Because it was polar!

Why did the firefly fail his entomology class?

He wasn't too bright.

Why did the chicken cross the möbius strip?

To get to the same side.

Biolo-jest

What do you call a biologist's self-portrait?

a cell-fie

What's the difference between a dog and a marine biologist?

One wags a tail and the other tags a whale.

What did one DNA strand say to the other?

"Stop copying me!"

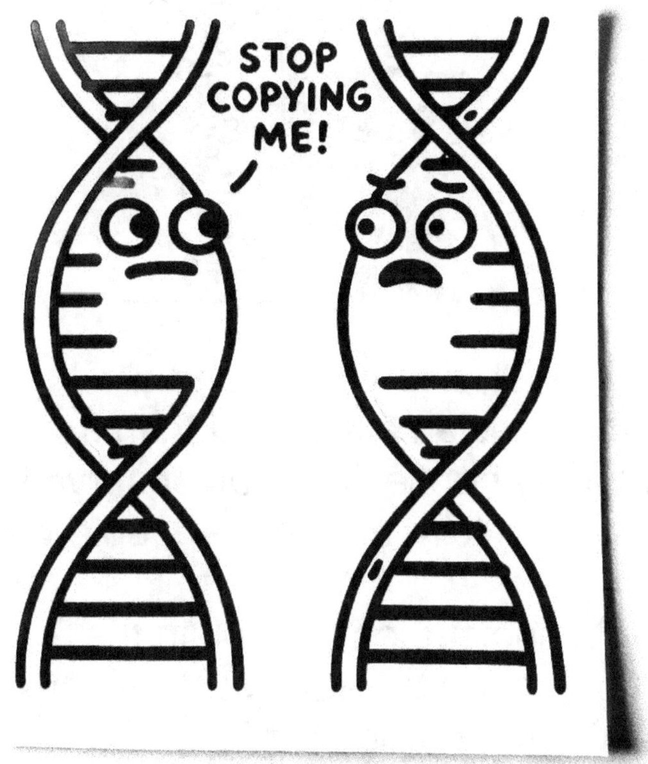

What did the biologist wear to impress his date?

Designer genes.

What's a biologist's favorite instrument?

a cell-o

A biologist, a physicist, and a mathematician are standing in front of an empty house. They all observe two people walk in, and three people walk out.
The biologist tries to explain the phenomenon by stating, "Well, they must have reproduced."
The physicist offers a different explanation, "There must have been an error in measurement."
Then, the mathematician says, "If one more person walks in, the house will be empty again."

Why do molecular biologists look forward to Fridays?

They can wear genes to work.

What do you call it when your biology teacher lowers your grade?

bio-degraded

Why did the physicist break up with the biologist?

There was no chemistry.

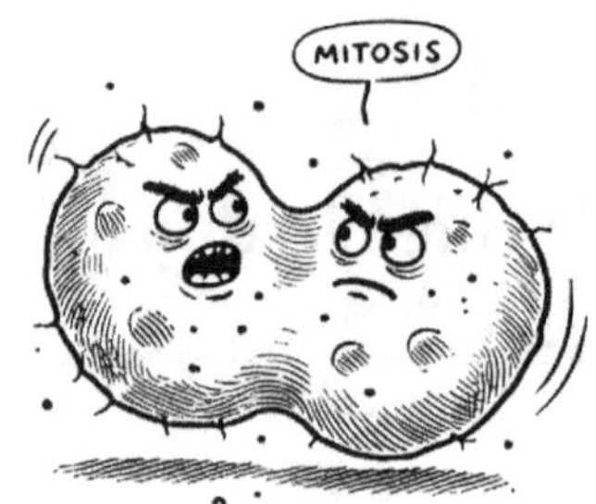

We really need to stop talking about mitosis.

It's such a divisive issue.

Blinded With Science

What did the thermometer say to the graduated cylinder?

"You may have graduated, but I have more degrees."

What did the science book say to the math book?

You've got problems.

Why did the science teacher throw a
temper tantrum?

She reached her boiling point.

How often do scientists look at the table
of elements?

periodically

Why did the scientist bring string to the lab?

He wanted to tie up some loose ends regarding a certain theory.

My girlfriend told me I was average.

She is so mean!

Carbon Dating

Did you know that oxygen went on a
date with potassium?

Yeah, it went OK.

Are you made of Copper and Tellurium?

Because you are CuTe!

When Oxygen and Magnesium started
dating, I was all like,

"OMg!"

Why didn't the skeleton go to the ball?

Because it had no body to go with.

Two blood cells met and fell in love.

Alas, it was all in vein.

How does a scientist freshen her breath?

experi-mints

Cosmic Comedy

What are the two reasons for eating light?

If you're on a diet or if you're a black hole.

How do you throw a successful party in space?

You planet.

How does the universe always manage
to throw the best parties?

It invites all the stars.

How does the moon cut its hair?

Eclipse it.

Do you like Orion's belt?

Yeah, I give it three stars.

What kinds of books do planets usually
like to read?

comet books

How do you know that Saturn has been married multiple times?

Because she has a lot of rings!

What kind of music do planets dance to?

Nep-tunes

What's an astronaut's favorite key on
the keyboard?

the space bar

Where do astronauts leave their
spaceships?

at parking meteors

Did you hear about the restaurant on the Moon?

The food was out of this world, but there was no atmosphere.

How do astronauts serve lunch in zero gravity?

on flying saucers

Einstein developed a theory about space.

It was about time, too.

What did Earth say to Mars when it got irritated?

Get a life!!

Elementary My Dear Watson

Where did the chemist have his lunch?

on a periodic table

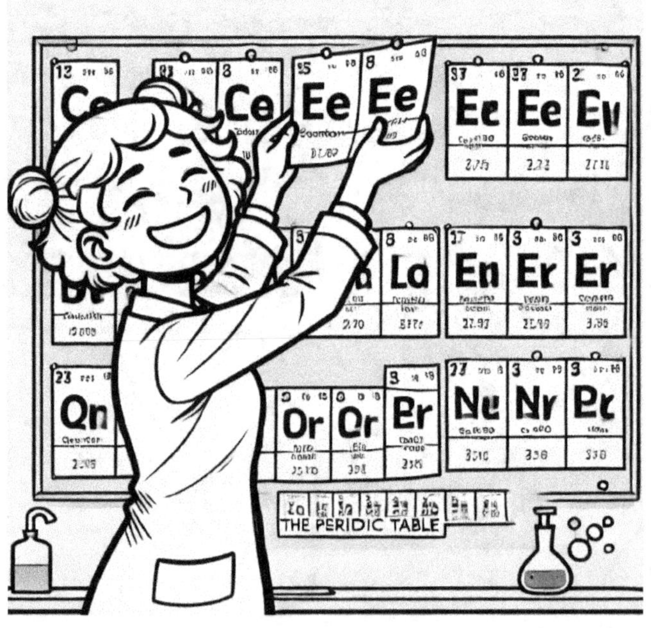

Why did the chemist hang up periodic table posters everywhere?

It made her feel like she was in her element.

What's a pirate's favorite element?

aaarrrgon

What do you do with a sick scientist?

Well, if you can't helium, and you can't curium, then you might as well barium.

How often are element jokes funny?

periodically

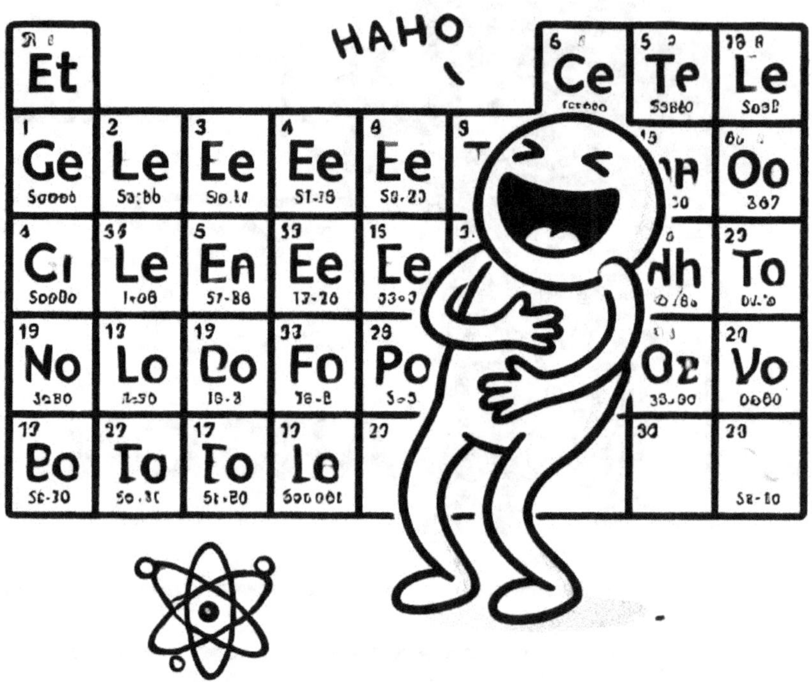

Did you hear about the singer named
Neil Coal?

His agent put a lot of pressure on him to
change his name to Neil Diamond.

H2Omg!!

What did one DNA say to the other DNA?

Do these genes make me look fat?

Why did the mushroom get invited to all the parties?

Because he was a fungi.

Two men walk into a bar. The first man says, "I'll have some H2O."

The second man says, "I'll have some H2O, too."

The second man soon died.

What does a marine biologist call a FISH with no eyes?

FSH

How did the oceanographer cut the sea
in half?

with a sea-saw

I'm reading a book on anti-gravity.

I can't put it down.

Illogically Geological

What did one tectonic plate say when it bumped into another?

"Sorry, my fault!"

What did the limestone say to the geologist?

Don't take me for granite! (That wasn't very gneiss.)

What happens when fossilized trees
watch scary movies?

They become petrified.

How do geologists ask each other out?

They say, "Are you a carbon sample?
Because I'd love to date you."

What kind of music shows do geologists like?

rock concerts

Why are mountains so funny?

Because they're hill areas.

Why did the geologist stop playing hide-and-seek with the mountain?

Because it always peaked.

What's a geologist's favorite type of music?

rock

Laughing in the Lab

Why did the germ cross the microscope?

to get to the other slide

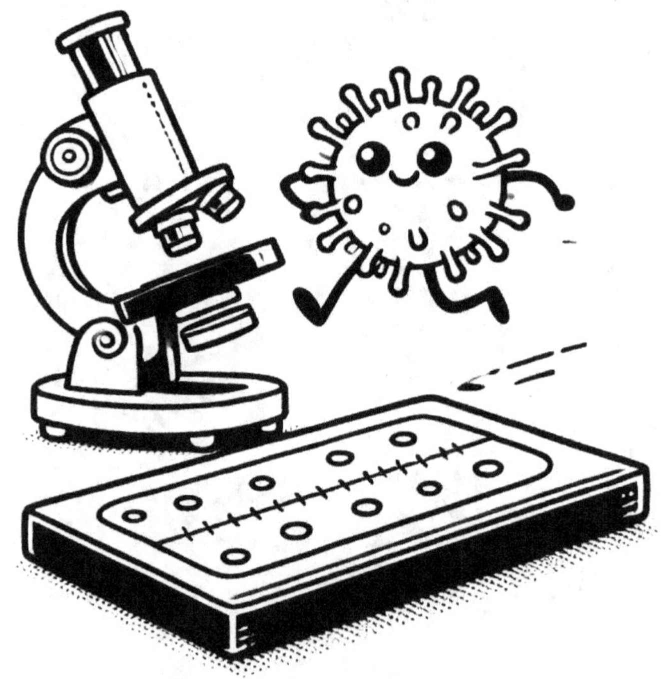

What do you call scientific research that rubs you the wrong way?

science friction

What's a scientist's favorite holiday song?

"Oh Chemis-TREE, oh Chemis-TREE!"

Why didn't the skeleton cross the road?

He didn't have the guts.

What do you call an acid with an attitude?

a-mean-o acid

An infectious disease walks into a bar. The barman says, "We don't serve your type here."

The disease replies, "Well you're not a very good host."

What do computer scientists like to eat?

chips

Which blood type is the most optimistic?

b positive

Quarky Humor

A Higgs Boson walks into a church. The priest says, "We don't allow Higgs Bosons in here."

The Higgs Boson says, "But without me how can you have mass?"

What does a subatomic duck say?

quark

The past, the present and the future all walk into a bar at the same time.

It was tense...

I have a new theory on inertia, but it doesn't seem to be gaining momentum....

A group of protesters form outside a science lab and start chanting... "What do we want?

Time Travel! When do we want it?

It's irrelevant!"

What did the angry proton say to the electron?

"I'm sick of your negativity."

What do protons and life coaches have in common?

They know how to stay positive.

Why did the neutron go to therapy?

It was having a meltdown.

What did the quantum physicist say to the stressed-out student?

"Don't worry, it's all relative."

What's a physicist's favorite exercise?

jumping to conclusions

Relatively Humorous

A neutron walks into a bar and orders a drink. When the barman gives it to him, he asks, "How much?"

The barman replies, "For you-no charge."

Why did the scientist take out his doorbell?

He wanted to win the no-bell prize.

A photon checks into a hotel. The bellhop asks, "Can I help you with your luggage?"

It replies, "I don't have any. I'm travelling light."

Why does the physics professor study gravity?

It keeps her grounded.

What kind of tree can fit into your hand?

a palm tree

What did the helpless T-Cell say when
facing the infection?

"Is there antibody out there?"

What is a tornado's favorite game to play?

Twister

What do solids, liquids and gases all have in common?

They all matter!